Kids find ways to make where we live a better place. Kids care about our earth. Kids care about each other. So, kids work hard to make a difference.

1

Many grown ups have done important things to make a difference.

Mohandas Gandhi helped to make people free.

Dr. Martin Luther King, Jr. helped all people to be treated fairly.

Mother Teresa helped the poor and the sick.

But you do not have to be a grown up to make a difference. Kids can do it, too.

A hurricane hit the island of Puerto Rico. The storm wiped out many trees. Some kids wanted to help. They planted new trees.

There are many ways to help.
These kids saw trash near their
home. They got together. They
picked up trash so the plants and
animals can grow.

Kids in New Jersey learned that birds were losing their homes. They wanted to help the birds.

The New Jersey class made calendars. Then they sold them. The boys and girls used the money to make homes for birds.

Some kids in Tennessee wanted to help the birds, too. They made posters asking for trees. People gave them trees. They planted the trees for the birds.

You can make a difference, too. Clean up a messy park. Water a tree. Make a poster.

There are many things for you to do. You will feel proud when you make a difference!